Praise for RelationSHIPS

Reading *RelationSHIPS* was like sitting down with wise friends who understand both Scripture and real life. Jon and Teresa Harper have written something that speaks straight to the heart—practical, honest, and full of grace. Their look at Samson's story through these seven "ships" opened my eyes to what healthy, God-honoring relationships can look like. This book reminded me that living in the right relationship—with God and with others—isn't just possible, it's essential. I'm grateful for the encouragement and clarity it brought to my own life, and I know it will do the same for you.

Dr. Grant Byrd, Student Ministry Associate, Southern Baptists of Texas Convention, TexasYouthGuy.com

RelationSHIPS is both a creative and convicting guide that points us back to the heart of God in how we love and lead others. Through a powerful SHIP metaphor and meaningful parallels to Samson's story, Jon and Teresa connect timeless biblical truth to the struggles we all face in our relationships. You can feel their heart on every page, shaped by years of ministry and a steady walk with the Lord. This book is honest, relatable, and anchored in truth. It is a must-read for anyone seeking to grow in faith and connection.

Melissa Eickenhorst, Entrepreneur, High Performance Coach, Host of *The Ambition Coalition* Podcast

Jon and Teresa Harper don't just write about relationships; they live them well. This book is soaked in Scripture and shaped by years of real-life ministry and honest conversations. It's not about quick fixes or surface-level advice. It's about learning to love God, love others, and even love yourself in ways that reflect Christ. Every chapter points you back to the only anchor that truly holds—Jesus. Whether you're in calm waters or facing something challenging, *RelationSHIPS* offers practical, encouraging, and hope-rooted wisdom. I know Jon and Teresa personally—they are the real deal. Their words come from lived-out faith and deep compassion, and this book is an extension of their calling to help others grow.

David Cook, Care Pastor at First Baptist, Atlanta, GA

In *RelationSHIPS*, Jon and Teresa Harper invite readers to take an honest look at the connections that shape their lives—from their relationship with God to their relationships with others. With transparency and authenticity, they share their own struggles and triumphs, offering a refreshing reminder that growth often comes through both failure and faith. Using the life of Samson as a powerful and relatable case study, he helps readers see how choices, character, and surrender go hand in hand for success. Each chapter is rich with biblical insight and practical application, and the included reflection questions make it perfect for personal study or small group discussion. This book is a valuable guide for anyone seeking to strengthen communication and build deeper relationships that honor God.

Ava Bates, Executive Pastor at The Light Church, Willis, TX

Jon and Teresa Harper have done it again! They've taken on the complex topic of relationships and offered a deeply biblical perspective on what it means to live in relationship with others while growing in our walk with Jesus. What I love most about this book is what I've always appreciated about the Harpers: it isn't driven by feelings but grounded firmly in the Word of God. The biblical wisdom and insight found in these pages are exactly what I've come to expect from them. I highly recommend this book to anyone seeking to deepen their relationships and strengthen their faith.

Jeff Bachman, Regional Director, Colorado Baptist General Convention

Jon and Teresa Harper have written a masterpiece that speaks straight to the heart. *RelationSHIPS* captures their genuine passion for helping others grow closer to God and each other through practical wisdom and biblical insight. Their words are authentic, transparent, and full of life lessons. The Anchor Points, Ship Logs, and Crew Talks are fantastic ways to engage the reader. This insight obviously comes from the Harper's years of ministry and walking faithfully with the Lord. This book doesn't just teach about relationships—it invites you to experience God's design for them. Do yourself a favor, read this book and pass it on to your personal relationships, you won't regret it! I highly recommend it to anyone who desires to strengthen their faith and navigate life's waters with grace and purpose.

Tyson King, President and Founder of Iron Bluffs Christian Camp and Inspire Financial Group

RelationSHIPS is an insightful and thought-provoking book that takes readers on a journey about relationships using the imagery of ships and the Biblical story of Samson. With a blend of personal stories and biblical content, Jon and Teresa have written *RelationSHIPS* to help us navigate personal relationships with authenticity and purpose. Whether you're seeking to strengthen a marriage, heal after conflict, or build deeper friendships, *RelationSHIPS* offers a roadmap for deeper relationships. Because I have known Jon and Teresa for over a decade and have seen them be very relational with campers, group leaders, and FUGE Camps staff, I can recommend this book to anyone who wants to understand how relationships work and what steps are needed to keep them strong.

Joe Hicks, Manager, FUGE Camps

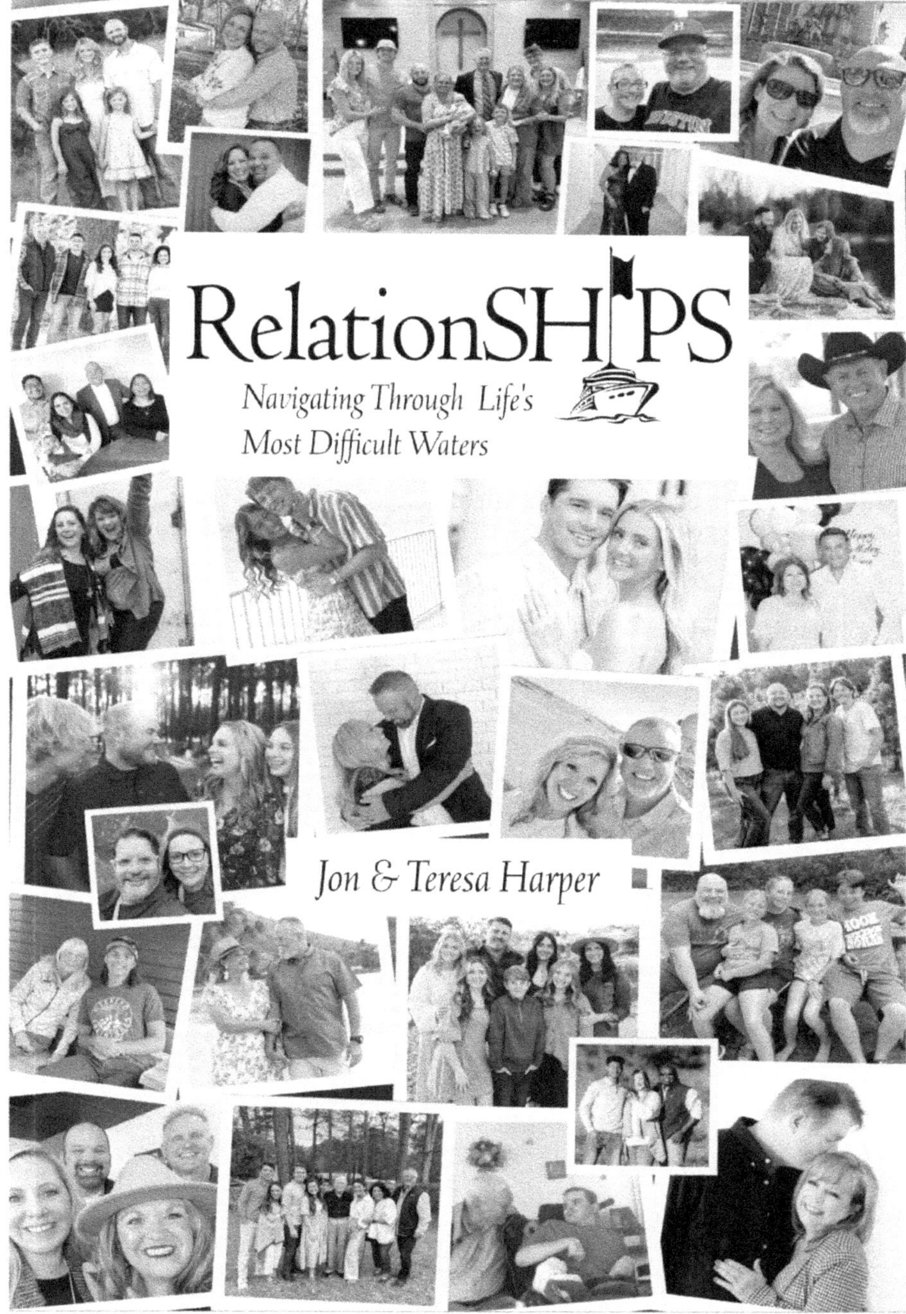
RelationSHIPS
Navigating Through Life's
Most Difficult Waters
Jon & Teresa Harper

Every effort has been made to ensure that all the information in this book is accurate at the time of publication. If you have questions or comments about this book or need information about special sales or bulk purchases, please contact Harvest Creek Publishing & Design at info@harvestcreek.net.

First Edition
ISBN: 978-1-961641-46-4

Jon & Teresa Harper
The WORD Ministries
PO Box 613, Willis, TX 77378
Phone: 713-417-2997 Email: admin@thewordministries.net
www.thewordministries.net

Book Cover & Layout by Harvest Creek Publishing & Design

Printed in the United States

Contents

Dedication

This book is first and foremost dedicated to **God**, the Creator of all things and the Author of every relationship. He designed us for connection and, through His Word, has given us truth, wisdom, and clarity to understand what healthy and unhealthy relationships look like. His Scriptures remain our compass, guiding us through every season and every storm.

We also dedicate this book to our **parents**, who taught us from an early age to turn to God's Word as the ultimate source of authority for life and faith. Their example and instruction laid the foundation for who we are and how we navigate relationships today.

To our children: **Lexi, Wade, and Dylan**, you are one of God's greatest gifts to us. Our prayer is that you will always put Jesus first in your lives, in your marriages, and in every relationship you carry. May you seek His direction, trust His Word, and follow His leading wherever He calls you. And to the loves of your lives, **Ryan, Faith, and Krystal,** we are so blessed to have you in our lives and look forward to having amazing family gatherings over the years. May you always feel loved and accepted in our family. We hope to be the best in-laws you could ever wish for.

And to our precious little **Ronin**. May you learn to seek the Lord and His plan for your life. God has beautiful plans for you, and part of that is loving family relationships. We pray that we will always foster that and set a great example for you to follow.

Finally, this book is dedicated to the **friends and family** who have poured into us over the years and to those who have encouraged us, prayed for us, spoken truth from God's Word, and lived out examples of faith before us. Your influence has helped shape our journey, and we are forever grateful.

Proverbs 3:5-6 NIV says, "Trust in the LORD with all your heart and lean not on your own understanding; in all your ways submit to him, and he will make your paths straight." May God continue to lead and guide all of us as we seek Him and trust Him in our earthly relationships.

Acknowledgments

Writing a book about *RelationSHIPS* means acknowledging the many people who have helped keep our ships afloat—sometimes by offering wisdom, sometimes by correcting our course, and occasionally by grabbing us by the collar and steering us away from the rocks.

FROM JON

-To Teresa: Thank you for standing by my side all these years with the patience of Job... and then some. Thank you for challenging me to be the spiritual leader and head of our home, while faithfully serving as the *neck*—turning my head when I clearly don't know where I'm going (which is often, because I am genuinely directionally challenged). Thank you for your unconditional love, your Christ-like grace toward people who are hard to love, and your constant reminder of what grace looks like in real relationships. You are the creative genius behind everything we do in ministry, and I remain convinced God custom-designed you specifically to handle me.

-To Dad (Jon): Thank you for being the ultimate example of how to love people well. Your gentle spirit has shaped the way I view manhood, leadership, and faith. Thank you for dragging me to church all those years so I could learn the Scriptures—and then actually live them out as an adult. I am who I am today because you lived what you taught.

FROM TERESA

-To Jon: Thank you for being the most incredible, godly man I could have ever asked for. You are an amazing husband, father, and friend. I am deeply grateful that God gave you the ability to write, because I am 100% a math brain, and words do not come naturally to me. It still amazes me how you can sit down and produce a book, a devotional, or a sermon in minutes. You are one of the smartest and most dedicated people I know. You always make me feel loved, protected, and cared for. Thank you for keeping me on time and punctual—without you, this book might still be just an idea scribbled somewhere (and probably late)!

-To Mom (Susan): Thank you for having a heart as big as Texas. Your generosity, encouragement, and unwavering belief in me—especially during my very rebellious teenage years—shaped who I am today. Thank you for seeing potential in me even when my life choices suggested otherwise.

-To Mary and Paul Whitaker: Mary, since you are my sister, I have probably learned more about relationships from you than anyone else. Thank you for not killing me when I was younger—especially when I called you a "Bible banger" and a "Jesus freak" while you were just trying to live out your faith. And Paul, thank you for being Jon's favorite family member. You earned it. The two of you mean the world to us.

FROM JON AND TERESA

We are incredibly thankful for the couples who have poured into our lives and taught us how to navigate relationships—even when the waters were anything but calm.

-To Greg and Mary Lea Dunn: Thank you for the incredible blessing you have been in our lives for over 25 years. You've walked with us through seasons of ministry in multiple churches, endured long stretches of life lived miles apart, and shared the adventure (and chaos) of raising families side by side. Along the way, there's been endless laughter, a few tears, plenty of spirited conversations, and more memories than we could ever count. Through every season—good, hard, and everything in between—your friendship has remained steady, faithful, and full of joy. We are deeply grateful not only to serve in ministry with you, but also to do life with you. Best friends forever... and yes, we mean that literally.

-To Steve and Donna Gantt: Thank you for the countless hours of counsel, leadership, and love. Thank you for treating us like your own children, mentoring us faithfully, and occasionally wanting to come through the phone to spank us. We needed it. Thank you for always pointing us back to God's Word. We would not be where we are today without you two. Thank you for always believing in us and encouraging us to meet our goals and strive for our dreams.

-To David and Jill Reaves: To our Branson buddies, thank you for always being there to make us laugh, smile, and remember that joy is essential in any relationship. We've learned so much from you, often without realizing it until later.

-To Jeff and Tammy Bachman: Your faithfulness to the Lord is a constant example to us. We wish you lived closer so we could spend more time together, because you make us better. Let's bring back some old-school Colorado mission trips soon.

-To James and Sheila Patrick: This book says, *"Forgiveness is the anchor of the Ship of Commitment,"* and no one has modeled that truth more clearly for us than you. Thank you for walking through life with us and showing us what real, biblical forgiveness looks like.

-To Shane and Jaclyn Denson: Thank you for supporting our ministry and all our not-so-normal ideas without hesitation. Your encouragement and faithfulness mean more than you know, and even though we don't talk every day, we know that you guys are friends who will always be there for us.

-To Ron and Ava Bates: Thank you for setting an example of bold faith for those in our community to follow. We are blessed to call you family, and we are so thankful that such incredible leaders are mentoring our daughter.

-To Brian and Chrystal Reynolds: Your friendship is invaluable to us, and we have enjoyed watching you guys grow in your faith. Thank you for always being there for us.

-To Casey and Bri Delay: You are basically a friend magnet, and your kids are watching firsthand what real, meaningful friendships are supposed to look like.

We are also deeply grateful for the many friends who have modeled healthy, faith-filled relationships for us. This is a short list, but honestly, it could go on and on and on.

-To David and Amy Cook, Jonathan and Heather Smith, Sherman and Tammy Aten, Willie and Melissa Eickenhorst, Grant and Jill Byrd, Tyson and Jacky King, Joe and Michelle Hicks, Jerry and Leslie Roberts, Jonathan and Ellyn Hewett, Jaime and Claudia Garcia, JJ and Fernanda Lopez, and Dustin and Erin Byrd: You are all amazing leaders who are impacting lives across America through your different forms of ministry. We want you to know you have made an impact on us, and we hope you like your picture on the book's cover.

-**To our children: Lexi, Wade, and Dylan:** Thank you for years of love, laughter, and an endless supply of sermons and book illustrations. You have taught us far more than we could ever teach you. We are so thankful that you have each found the loves of your lives, and we are incredibly blessed to welcome them into our family. We love you, **Ryan, Faith, and Krystal.**

-To Jesus Christ: Thank You for giving us eternal life and for dying on the cross for our sins. Our purpose on this earth is to know You and to make You known to a lost and dying world. Thank You for offering us the greatest gift of all, a relationship with God through Your death, burial, and resurrection.

Foreword

RELATIONSHIPS ARE AN integral part of our life's journey. And that journey is rarely a straight course. Our interactions with people are as unpredictable as a ship at sea. Sometimes our relationships move forward and grow stronger each day. At other times, we may be thrown off course when unforeseen issues disrupt our lives.

A valuable piece of advice I once received was, "Relationships evolve as people evolve." It is essential to continue forward, even during life's hardships, to sustain our relationships.

As people grow in greater self-awareness, insight, and maturity along life's way, their interpersonal relationships also improve. I can say with certainty that this has proven true in my life. My relationships, from childhood friends to colleagues and my spouse, have significantly shaped my personal growth over the years.

Webster's defines a relationship (/rəˈlāSHənˌSHip/) as how two or more people are connected or interrelated. It involves the way individuals interact and behave toward one another. Two people meet as strangers. However, their rapport grows and becomes a mutual bond through talking, shared experiences, and laughter. This bond advances through both collective momentum and individual growth.

So, I'll say it again: Relationships are an integral part of life. It's hard to avoid interacting with people unless you live under a rock (*and that seems a little uncomfortable*!). We need interaction with others to progress. Our evolution depends on our commitment *to* and acceptance *by* those around us.

But, being prone to sin, we often sabotage even our closest relationships because of our own wrongdoings. Our associations with others degrade because sin causes us to regress or decline personally. As a result, our connections with others suffer. A complete reset is often the only way to repair the trust, communication, and vulnerability that our imperfections have harmed.

In this book, Jon and Teresa Harper examine relationships through the lens of the prominent Bible figure, Samson. He was a man known for his extraordinary strength and his famously long, uncut hair. Upon his miraculous birth, Samson was consecrated by God as a Nazirite and was called to be a judge for his nation. The Word says that as Samson grew, the "Spirit of the LORD began to stir him." [Judges 13:25 NIV] *Wow! What a great way to start one's life.*

Still, Samson's life presented a series of contradictions. Though divinely appointed for God's work, Samson struggled with his sinful desires and often succumbed to temptation. He was the consummate "three steps forward, two steps backward" kind of guy. Always moving ahead, then regressing. We can all relate to this, whether or not we're ready to admit it.

Each time Samson consciously chose sin (regression), God still managed to advance His purposes through him (forward progress). It is interesting that, although he was definitely a man of the flesh, Samson still made it into the proverbial Hall of Faith according to Hebrews 11:32. We can learn a lot by examining Samson's life.

That's why I thoroughly enjoyed this book! Each chapter shows how Samson's imperfect experiences hold lessons for us about fulfilling God's will in how we treat others. Following the advice here will lead to increased personal growth and divine connections with others.

You'll enjoy taking a ride on the various relation*SHIPS* that move us toward powerful interactions with family, friends, coworkers, and others. Oh, and the chapter-to-chapter movement of the ship icon is something I think you'll really connect with, since it serves as a reminder of our own life's journey toward Heaven.

It's a true blessing to observe the beneficial effect God's presence has had on the Harpers' ministry and their work in strengthening relationships. Having known them throughout the years, I see that they are committed to being used by God in everything they put their hand to. Be blessed by the wisdom shared in this book as you strive to move forward in love with the people that the Lord has placed in your path.

Teresa Granberry

Author, Publisher, Friend

Introduction

LIFE IS OFTEN compared to a journey, and like any journey, it requires vessels to carry us along the way. For centuries, ships have served as powerful metaphors for adventure, discovery, danger, and purpose. Each ship is carefully crafted with a destination in mind, designed not to remain idle in the harbor but to set sail, endure storms, and reach distant shores.

In the same way, our relationships—with God, with others, and even with ourselves—can be seen as ships. Some ships are sturdy, guiding us toward meaningful destinations. Others drift aimlessly, damaged by storms or neglected in port. But every ship, whether seaworthy or struggling, tells a story about how we navigate the waters of life.

I've (Jon) experienced this firsthand in seasons where friendships that once felt solid began to drift apart. I would be left wondering if I had failed as a friend or if the tides of life had simply pulled us in different directions. At work, I've had coworkers I trusted suddenly turn against me, and those moments felt like leaks in my vessel that left me weary and discouraged. Even in my closest relationships with loved ones, I've faced storms—misunderstandings, disappointments, and times when we weren't on the same course. Each of these moments has reminded me that relationships require constant care, repair, and reliance on God's guidance to endure the rough waters and make it safely to shore.

This book explores seven essential "ships" that shape who we are and how we relate to others:

- Calling
- Catch
- Counsel
- Concealment
- Constraint
- Commitment
- Clean Slate

Each chapter looks at one of these ships through the lens of Scripture—highlighting the story of Samson in the book of Judges. Samson's life was filled with potential, yet often derailed by choices, temptations, and misplaced priorities. His journey serves as both a warning and a guide for us. Through his victories and failures, we see how God's purposes can still shine through even when our own strength falters. In the end, Samson reminds us that no matter how broken a vessel may seem, God is able to restore, redirect, and use it for His glory.

As we step into these pages, imagine yourself as a crew member on board. Every ship requires attention, discipline, and direction. Some days, the waters are calm; other days, the storm threatens to sink us. But in every season, God calls us to set sail with Him—trusting His design, following His voice, and fulfilling the purpose for which we were created.

⚓ Anchor Point

For we are his workmanship,
created in Christ Jesus for good works,
which God prepared ahead of time for us to do.
EPHESIANS 2:10, CSB

This book isn't just about information; it's about transformation. Each chapter will invite you to reflect, to pray, and to take steps toward strengthening your relationships. Along the way, you'll find biblical truths (Anchor Points), journaling prompts (Ship Logs), and discussion questions (Crew Talk) to help you stay on course. Be sure to utilize these action steps to fully experience the learning God wants you to have through this book.

You will notice that the ship in each chapter heading moves along the waves as the book progresses. We (Jon and Teresa) recommend that you read each chapter in succession, building upon the teachings contained therein. If we take these "ships" to heart, we will have better relationships with others.

So, take hold of the wheel. Loosen the ropes. Lift the anchor. It's time to launch into deeper waters and discover the relationSHIPS God has prepared for you.

ONE

The Ship of **CALLING**

IMAGINE A SHIP that doesn't carry cargo or passengers. It just sits in the harbor or at the dock day in and day out and never goes out on the water. It may seem both illogical and impractical that the very purpose for which a ship was designed, or the intentions of the one who carefully crafted it, would ultimately go unfulfilled, leaving its potential unrealized and its capabilities wasted. In essence, that ship didn't fulfill its calling.

A ship was never meant to remain docked indefinitely; its very design and purpose demand movement. It is built to sail, to navigate vast waters, and to fulfill the mission for which it was created. Likewise, its crew is not meant to remain idle. Still, it is called to a specific purpose, working together to ensure the ship reaches its intended destination.

In the same way, you and I were not meant to stay stagnant in life. We are created for movement, growth, and purpose, each of us with a unique journey to embark on and a destination to reach.

What Is a Calling?

You may think, "What is a calling? And who is calling me?" Your calling is your purpose. It's the inner passion that you can't stop thinking about. It's the thing you love doing—not because you feel forced, but because it brings joy and fulfillment. It's the sense that what you're doing is the very thing that makes life meaningful.

Many people live their entire lives without ever discovering why they were created. But you have been wired with specific gifts, abilities, and talents designed to bless others. Mark Twain once said,

The two most important days in your life
are the day you are born
and the day you find out why.
MARK TWAIN

Maybe you're called to coach a Little League team that will influence future generations. Perhaps you have a deep desire to create a charity that helps those facing life-threatening issues. But chances are, cost, uncertainty, fear of failure, or outside opinions have kept you from venturing out and taking the plunge. I know because I've wrestled with those very same barriers—wondering if I had enough resources, enough experience, or even enough courage to step into what God was placing on my heart.

The truth is, almost every meaningful calling comes with moments of hesitation and doubt. Still, those moments are often where God does His greatest work. When we learn to trust Him in the unknown, we discover that our limitations are actually opportunities for His strength to be revealed. What feels like a storm meant to sink us can instead become the very wind that propels our ship forward if we're willing to lift the sails and follow His lead.

My Story: Wrestling with God's Call

For me (Jon), the call came early. My first sense of God calling me to ministry came when I was a teen attending a youth camp. It wasn't just a fleeting thought; it was a deep, unmistakable stirring in my heart that I couldn't shake. But instead of embracing it, I pushed it aside. At that time, sports were my entire identity, primarily football. I lived and breathed the game, and the dream of playing at the highest level consumed my thoughts day and night.

I trained harder, played longer, and set my focus on becoming someone that others would admire. I had convinced myself that I was going to be the first offensive lineman on the cover of the Madden Football Game. The idea of walking away from that pursuit to follow God's call felt like giving up everything I thought made me valuable. Besides, all the ministers I knew were poor and had cars that smelled like chicken nuggets.

So, for the next five years, I ran. I ran by throwing myself deeper into football, by filling my schedule with practices, games, and goals that had nothing to do with ministry. I thought if I could achieve success on the field, the ache in my heart for something more would eventually go away. But it didn't. In fact, the harder I ran, the more restless I became. I didn't realize at the time that my striving was really a form of resistance against the One who had already written a greater story for me.

Then came the moment that changed everything. It was during what seemed like an ordinary pickup basketball game—nothing special, nothing extraordinary. And yet, in an instant, it became the turning point of my life. I went up for a lay-up, when I came down, someone landed on my ankle, and it shattered.

The ligament detached from the bone, and I suffered an injury that required major surgery. With it, my pro dreams collapsed overnight. All the years of training, sacrifice, and ambition suddenly felt like they had been ripped away from me. I was devastated. I remember lying in a hospital bed, angry, confused, and broken, asking God, "Why?"

But it was in that very brokenness that God finally got my attention. When I had nothing left to hold on to, I realized that what I had been running from was not meant to take life away from me—it was meant to give me life. Slowly, I began to see that God wasn't stripping me of fulfillment; He was offering me a plan that, if I committed to it, would lead to a life more meaningful than I ever could have dreamed on my own.

That realization didn't erase the pain overnight, but it opened my heart to surrender. And in that hospital bed, I told God that if he would just let me walk again, I would serve him with my life. I was blessed to go on and play four years of college football, making a difference on the field, but also in ministry.

It's been over 30 years since I said "Yes" to God's calling for my life. And since then, I've been serving in ministry for nearly three decades, serving side by side with my wife, Teresa. We have traveled speaking at youth camps, revivals, men's and women's retreats, and marriage conferences, fulfilling this calling in over 30 states, ministering to thousands of people, and watching God change lives in real and powerful ways.

Looking back, I can see that God's call never left me—He was waiting for me to surrender. And once I did, I found joy, purpose, and fulfillment far beyond anything I had planned for myself. I never made it onto the cover of a Madden Football Game. But I have made a difference in other people's lives for eternity by being a willing vessel that God chose to share the gospel.

Samson's Call

There's a story found in the Bible about a man named Samson, whose journey is recorded in the book of Judges and begins with his miraculous birth. His parents had long been unable to conceive, which in their culture carried deep shame and sorrow. Then, in the midst of their despair, the Angel of the Lord appeared to his mother with an astounding announcement:

"Although you are unable to conceive
and have no children,
you will conceive and give birth to a son.
Now please be careful not to drink wine or beer,

[cont'd next page]

or to eat anything unclean; for indeed,
you will conceive and give birth to a son.
You must never cut his hair,
because the boy will be a Nazirite to God from birth,
and he will begin to save Israel
from the power of the Philistines."
JUDGES 13:3B-5, CSB

From the very beginning, Samson's life was marked by divine purpose. His parents were entrusted with the weighty responsibility of raising a child set apart for God—a Nazirite, dedicated wholly to the Lord in both appearance and lifestyle. The Nazirite vow was a sacred commitment described in the Law of Moses (Numbers 6), and it involved three key requirements: abstaining from wine or anything that came from the vine, never cutting one's hair, and avoiding contact with anything dead. Each of these restrictions served as a physical reminder that the person belonged completely to God and was to live differently from the world around them.

Samson's calling was clear: he was to be God's chosen instrument to deliver Israel from the oppressive grip of the Philistines. But as Samson grew older, the tension between his calling and his cravings became painfully obvious. He was blessed with extraordinary strength and influence. Yet, time and again, he chose to pursue his own passions rather than God's plan. Though he had the potential to impact an entire nation, his personal desires—whether for recognition, pleasure, or relationships that pulled him away from God—consistently outweighed his higher purpose. His story is both inspiring and heartbreaking, reminding us that great potential can be squandered when *self* takes priority over *surrender.*

The Caller and the Calling

Just like Samson, each of us was created for a purpose. And just like in any mission—whether in the military, a business, or a sports team—there is someone who issues the orders. Scripture makes it clear who our Caller is:

For we are his workmanship,
created in Christ Jesus for good works,
which God prepared ahead of time for us to do.
EPHESIANS 2:10, CSB

The word "workmanship" can also be translated as "masterpiece." That means you're not an accident. You were designed with care, intentionally equipped with specific gifts that no one else can bring to the world. As chapter 11 in the book of Romans reminds us:

Regarding the gospel,
they are enemies for your advantage,
but regarding election,
they are loved because of the patriarchs,
since God's gracious gifts and calling are irrevocable.
ROMANS 11:28-29, CSB

In other words, your calling doesn't expire. You may ignore it, resist it, or run from it like I once did, but it will always be there, waiting for you to answer.

⚓ Anchor Point

Our Lord and God, you are worthy to receive
glory and honor and power,
because you have created all things,
and by your will they exist and were created.
REVELATION 4:11, CSB

🕮 Ship Log (Reflection)

Write about a time when you felt God nudging you toward something—an opportunity, conversation, or risk of faith. Did you follow His call or resist it? How did that choice shape you?

🗨 Crew Talk (Discussion)

Why do you think so many people ignore or resist God's calling? Share your thoughts with a friend or group and talk about how you can encourage one another to stay true to God's purpose.

The Port of Application

Recognize Your Caller.

Your calling comes from God, not from culture, family expectations, or personal ambition. Take time this week to pray: "Lord, remind me that my purpose is found in You alone."

Rediscover Your Passion.

Think about the activities, opportunities, or burdens that energize you. These are often clues to the unique ways God designed you to serve. Below, write at least two of your passions and reflect on *How might God use these in me for His glory?*

Release the Fear.

Fear of failure often keeps us docked in the harbor. Remember, ships weren't built for docks; they were built for seas. What is one step of faith you can take this week, even if it feels risky?

 Closing Prayer

Lord, thank You for creating me as Your workmanship—Your masterpiece. Forgive me for the times I've resisted Your calling or tried to pursue my own way. Give me the courage to untie from the dock of fear and to set sail into the waters of purpose You designed for me. Help me live for Your glory and use my gifts to bless others. In Jesus' name, Amen.

TWO

The Ship of **CATCH**

NOT EVERYTHING THAT looks good is from God. From Eden to Samson to our own lives today, the Ship of Catch reminds us that appearances can deceive, but God's purpose never does.

Hooked by Appearances

Years ago, we traveled to Florida for a conference. After checking into our hotel and unpacking, I wandered over to the window and looked over the Intracoastal Waterway. The pristine blue waters shimmered in the afternoon sun, reflecting streaks of light that danced across the surface like tiny diamonds. Boats of all sizes drifted lazily, but what grabbed my attention wasn't the scenery, it was the largest yacht I had ever laid eyes on. Towering above the other vessels, its sleek white hull and polished decks looked like something out of a magazine. The design was flawless, every line and angle crafted with precision, giving it an elegance that demanded to be noticed.

Later, we discovered that the yacht was owned by someone famous, which only added to its mystique. We couldn't help but daydream about what it would be like to step on board, to be invited on a ride across those sparkling waters, and to experience firsthand the luxury we could only admire from a distance. I never stepped on that yacht, never spoke to its crew, never even came close to being welcomed inside—yet it captured me. For several moments, I found myself completely mesmerized, staring at this magnificent vessel as if it carried some secret about life I didn't want to miss.

Samson knew that feeling. His eyes locked on something he wanted, and nothing else seemed to matter.

When he returned home,
he told his father and mother,
"A young Philistine woman in Timnah
caught my eye. I want to marry her . . .
Get her for me! She looks good to me."
JUDGES 14:2A, 3B, NLT

The moment Samson laid eyes on the Philistine woman, he wasn't interested in God's plan, his parents' counsel, or even the consequences of his choice. He was consumed by what appealed to him at that moment. His decision wasn't based on faith or obedience; it was based on sight and desire. Samson didn't choose God's purpose for him, but by what caught his eye. And like a ship lured off course by the shimmer of a distant shore, he set sail on the Ship of Catch—bound for disaster.

The tragic part is that this wasn't just a one-time mistake; it was a pattern in Samson's life, a recurring drift toward whatever looked good on the surface. But this lustful desire ultimately pulled him away from the calling God had placed on him. We will find out later in the book of Judges that Samson's ultimate demise came from a time when he let looks and appearances lure him into an unholy relationship that led him down a path of pain and suffering.

When Looks Deceive

The lure of what looks pleasurable or enticing affects many people today as well. People chase jobs because the salary looks good—only to discover that the long hours, relentless stress, and constant pressure slowly wreck their health, drain their joy, and fracture their families. Others get hooked by images and media that promise excitement but only distort God's design for intimacy, leaving hearts empty and relationships broken. The shiny new car or bigger house looks good at first glance. Still, the weight of monthly payments and unexpected expenses can quickly suffocate a family's budget and peace of mind.

Teens and young adults jump into relationships to avoid loneliness or to be seen as "having someone," only to end up hurt or compromising who God created them to be. Entrepreneurs rush into partnerships with people who look impressive on paper but lack integrity, and eventually watch their dreams unravel under the weight of betrayal. What looks good in the moment often closes our eyes to the long-term cost. The appearance sparkles, but the outcome? Regret, disappointment, and sometimes wounds that take years to heal.

Samson understood this all too well. Time and again, he chased after what looked good on the surface—whether it was relationships, recognition, or revenge—without pausing to consider God's purpose for his life. Just like us, he discovered that what "looked good" rarely led to what was good. His story is a sobering reminder that appearances can deceive, but God's calling is always steady and true.

Unfortunately, these patterns of destruction and Ship of Catch can be traced back all the way to Eden:

> *The woman saw that the tree was good for food*
> *and delightful to look at . . . So she took*
> *some of its fruit and ate it . . ..*
> GENESIS 3:6, CSB

From the very beginning, humanity has been drawn to what looks appealing but ultimately leads to regret. Eve reached for the fruit because it seemed good in the moment, just as Samson reached for relationships that seemed pleasing to the eye, and just as we often reach for jobs, possessions, or people that promise fulfillment but leave us empty.

The Ship of Catch is deceptive. It sails smoothly and looks shiny at first, but the further it drifts, the more it pulls us away from the safe harbor of God's design. What looks like opportunity can become captivity, and what looks like freedom can actually be the start of chains.

The Cost of Being Caught

The book of Proverbs warns us plainly:

There is a way that seems right to a person,
but its end is the way to death.
PROVERBS 14:12, CSB

Samson's life is a sobering example of this truth. He continually followed what looked right to his eyes instead of what was right in God's sight. Time after time, his desires pulled him off course, and nowhere is this more evident than in his encounter with Delilah.

AUTHOR'S NOTE: We recommend that readers who haven't experienced the full narrative of Samson's life pause now to read the book of Judges, Chapters 13-16, in the Bible. *You'll find Samson's entire life story, from his birth to his last moments, in these chapters. Reading this passage will give you a fuller understanding of how an anointed man of God went from "hero" to "prisoner." After that, you'll have a better grasp of Samson's relationship failures.*

Judges 16 tells us that Samson fell in love with a woman from the Valley of Sorek named Delilah. To Samson, she "looked good," just like the women before her (Judges 16:4–5). But what he didn't see was her heart. Delilah was not drawn to him out of love or devotion—she was drawn by greed. The Philistine rulers approached her and offered a staggering sum of money if she could uncover the secret of Samson's strength. Instead of protecting him, she allowed herself to be bought, trading loyalty for silver. Samson thought he had found love, but he had walked straight into a trap.

Temptation is never innocent; the hook is always baited. The outward appearance seems harmless, even appealing, but hidden beneath the surface is destruction. Samson's relationship with Delilah ended in betrayal, blindness, and bondage. After revealing his secret, he was captured, his eyes were gouged out, and he was forced to grind grain in prison like an animal. What looked good in the beginning cost him everything—his freedom, vision, and nearly his life. God's Word reminds us of this critical truth:

"Humans do not see what the LORD sees,
for humans see what is visible,
but the LORD sees the heart."
1 SAMUEL 16:7B, CSB

Samuel failed to learn this lesson in his own life. If Samson had looked past Delilah's beauty to discern her character, his story might have ended differently. But by trusting what he saw instead of what God saw, he paid the ultimate price.

Samson's downfall is a warning to us all. Temptation rarely looks dangerous; it often looks desirable. But every time we choose based on appearance alone, we risk being caught in something that leads to regret, loss, or even destruction. The Ship of Catch may look inviting, but its cost is far greater than the fleeting pleasure it promises.

Samson's story may feel distant, but the lessons hit close to home. Today, "Delilah" can take many forms—an opportunity that promises quick money but compromises integrity, a relationship that feels exciting but pulls us away from God, or the constant chase for approval and status that looks fulfilling but leaves us empty. Like Samson, we can be blinded by what looks good on the outside while ignoring the danger beneath the surface. The cost of being caught is still the same: regret, brokenness, and missed opportunities to walk in God's purpose. The enemy doesn't show us the chains up front; he just dangles the bait. That's why we must look deeper, asking God to help us see not only the appearance but the heart, so we don't fall into traps that look appealing but lead to bondage.

Escaping the Trap

Recognize the Enemy's Tactics.

Jesus made it clear:

A thief comes only to steal and kill and destroy.
I have come so that they may have life
and have it in abundance.
JOHN 10:10, CSB

The enemy is a master of disguise, dressing up destruction to look like delight. He knows how to bait the hook—using temptation, distractions, or opportunities that seem harmless but are meant to entangle us. Recognizing his tactics is the first step to escaping the trap. When we begin to see that behind every "quick fix" or too-good-to-be-true promise is an enemy trying to rob us of God's best, we can pause, resist, and cling to the abundant life Jesus offers.

Retrain Your Vision.

Paul urged believers:

> *Do not be conformed to this age, but be transformed by the renewing of your mind . . .*
> ROMANS 12:2A, CSB

The Ship of Catch sails strongest when we allow culture to shape our vision—when we let trends, appearances, or surface-level success define what's valuable. To retrain our vision means to see through the lens of Scripture, allowing God's Word and Spirit to renew how we think and what we desire. It's learning to look past the surface and discern the heart. When we let God reshape our perspective, we no longer settle for what looks good—we hunger for what is truly good.

The best way to transform your mind is by reading the Bible daily. Open God's Word and let it speak to you. God wants to change your thoughts and your beliefs to the ones that will lead you to honor and glorify Him.

Remember Gratitude.

Gratitude is one of the most powerful anchors God gives us. When appearances threaten to pull us out to sea, gratitude reminds us of what we already have and who God already is. Gratitude reframes our perspective, shifting our focus from what looks shiny and new to what God has already provided. It's hard to be deceived by appearances when our hearts are anchored in thanksgiving.

Gratitude steadies us, protects us from envy, and keeps us rooted in the truth that every good and perfect gift comes from above. When we practice gratitude, we trade the trap of chasing "what looks good" for the joy of resting in what *is* good—God's faithful provision and presence.

I (Teresa) grew up believing that I always had to be in a relationship. I didn't appreciate my single status or the valuable time I could have spent with God, free from relationship distractions. This led to a terrible pattern of unhealthy relationships that never genuinely satisfied or fulfilled me. My perception of "good" guided every decision I made.

It was until I went off to college that I realized Jesus was all I needed. True peace, which I had long sought, finally came to me when I entered a new reality of purpose, joy, and completeness in Christ.

⚓ Anchor Point

Do not love the world or the things in the world.

1 JOHN 2:15A, CSB

🕮 Ship Log (Reflection)

On the following page, write about a time you were "caught" by appearances. What did God teach you through that experience?

Crew Talk (Discussion)

What "baited hooks" are most common around you (e.g., money, popularity, relationships, social media)? How can we protect one another?

The Port of Application

Spot the Bait.

Where are you tempted to chase something because it looks good? Name it before God.

Study the Cost.

Journal about a decision that looked right but led to regret. What warning can you carry forward?

Settle Your Heart.

What practices renew your mind (Scripture memory, fasting from media, wise community)?

Shift Your Gaze.

Who or what do you compare yourself to most? How can gratitude reframe it?

Select Your Crew.

What boundary will you put in place this week to avoid being "caught?"

 Closing Prayer

Lord, I confess that I often chase what looks good instead of what is right. Give me Your eyes to see beyond appearances. Anchor me in Your truth. In Jesus' name, Amen.

THREE

The Ship of **COUNSEL**

WE'VE ALL MET the "walking Google"—that certain someone always ready to advise you on parenting, health, politics, and even tomorrow's weather. We even know people who never went to school to study meteorology but are experts in all things weather. We have been advised on health and wellness from people who are chronically ill and in desperate need of their own medical advice. Even well-meaning people have talked to us about political candidates, policies, and government, though they themselves have never held office or done much in the political sector.

For instance, if I were to give you golf advice, it would probably not lead you in the right direction because a good round of golf for me means I still have at least one ball left at the end of the day. The point is that all of us feel the need to give counsel and advice to people all the time. As we will see from Samson, the Ship of Counsel is necessary, but we must be careful about whom we are taking counsel from.

Samson's Ignored Counsel

When Samson told his parents he wanted a Philistine wife, they urged him toward a wiser path:

> *. . ."Can't you find a young woman among your relatives or among any of our people? Must you go to the uncircumcised Philistines for a wife?"*
> JUDGES 14:3A, CSB

But Samson replied:

> *"Get her for me. She's the right one for me."*
> JUDGES 14:3B, CSB

Wise counsel was offered but not heeded. Samson's parents weren't just being picky or narrow-minded; they were reminding him of God's clear command for Israel not to intermarry with the nations that worshiped other gods. They knew that such unions would lead to compromise and idolatry, pulling Samson away from his calling. Their words came from both love as parents and reverence for God's law, but Samson brushed them aside.

Instead of listening, Samson followed his own feelings. His response—"She's the right one for me"—reveals how easily our personal desires can drown out the voices of wisdom. He measured "right" by what pleased his eyes, not by what aligned with God's will. The tragedy is that ignoring counsel was not a one-time misstep for

Samson; it was part of a larger pattern of disregarding the guidance of others and ultimately the guidance of God.

Samson's denial of wisdom serves as a warning for us. God often places wise voices in our lives—parents, mentors, pastors, trusted friends—not to restrict us, but to protect us. Ignoring godly counsel can set us on a course that feels exciting at first but ends in regret. Listening may not always be easy, especially when it challenges our desires. But it can be the very thing that saves us from heartache and keeps us aligned with God's greater plan.

I (Teresa) know what it feels like to resist the advice of parents. As a teenager, I thought I knew better and didn't want to hear the warnings my mom and dad gave me. They would often remind me, "You are the company you keep." But I shrugged it off, convinced that I could handle myself and wouldn't be influenced.

Looking back, I see how wrong I was. The more time I spent with the wrong crowd, the more their choices became my choices, and before long, I found myself caught up in things that led to trouble and heartache. What I thought was freedom turned out to be a trap, and it took a lot of pain for me to realize my parents were right all along. They weren't trying to ruin my fun; they were trying to protect my future.

I'm so glad that when I went off to college, I turned back to the foundational truths of God's Word that my parents taught me. I actually stumbled upon a flyer for "FREE FOOD" at the Baptist Student Ministry (a Christian organization). I walked through the doors of that place, and God began doing miraculous work in my life. I finally found a friend group of people who would help me grow in my Christian faith and lead me to desire a closer relationship with Christ. I laid down all the sinful habits that I had been wallowing in and sought the Lord with all my heart. I realized that it's never too late to turn your life around, but it's also a lot easier when you have good people as your guide and your counsel.

⚓ Anchor Point

"Bad company corrupts good character."
1 CORINTHIANS 15:33B, NLT

Considering the Source

We live in a world overflowing with voices. Social media feeds, podcasts, influencers, friends, coworkers, and even family members are constantly speaking into our lives. Some voices shout, while others whisper subtly in the background. But the real question is this: Are they trustworthy? The book of Psalms gives us a clear filter:

How happy is the one
who does not walk in the advice of the wicked
or stand in the pathway with sinners
or sit in the company of mockers!
PSALM 1:1, CSB

Not every voice deserves equal weight. Some will guide us closer to God's purpose, while others will slowly pull us off course.

In order to stay on the right path, we must be discerning. We should readily know the answers to these questions:

- Who am I listening to?
- Do their lives reflect the outcomes I want for myself?
- If someone is constantly negative, cynical, or chasing empty pursuits, why would I expect their advice to lead me toward joy and fulfillment?

On the other hand, when we listen to people who are walking faithfully with God, we often find their words carry the wisdom, encouragement, and perspective we need. Scripture reminds us that both the path we choose and the voices we follow ultimately shape where we end up.

Samson's parents gave him no reason to doubt their guidance. From what we can see, they had a strong marriage and were faithful in honoring and seeking the Lord. Yet Samson refused to listen. Convinced he knew better, he ignored their counsel, and the consequences were devastating.

We face the same challenge today. Voices surround us—social media influencers, celebrities, friends, coworkers, and countless others—each one offering their opinions and urging us to follow their lead. Some voices sound appealing, but not all are trustworthy. That's why it's crucial to pause and consider the source. Does this voice align with God's Word? Does it lead me closer to Him or further away?

Samson's story invites us to ask those hard questions before we act. Because in the end, the voices we choose to follow will either guide us into God's purpose or steer us toward regret. Who are you allowing to speak into your life—and where are they leading you?

A humbling flip side is to ask, "Would I take counsel from myself?" That question forces us to examine whether our own lives are marked by wisdom, humility, and obedience to God. Or whether we're just giving out opinions rooted in personal preference and pride.

The truth is: People are watching us, too. If our words don't line up with the fruit of our lives, why would anyone take our advice seriously? Considering the source isn't just about evaluating others—it's also about allowing God to shape us into a source of counsel others can trust.

Considering the Significance

Ignoring sound counsel set Samson on a path toward bondage and blindness. His downfall didn't happen overnight—it resulted from repeatedly choosing his own desires over the wisdom of those who loved him and the commands of the God who had called him.

Every day, we face the same choice: "Which voices will I elevate in my life?" Not everyone who is near you is for you, and not everyone who speaks into your situation has your best interest—or God's will—at heart. The book of Proverbs teaches:

> *Without guidance, a people will fall,*
> *but with many counselors there is deliverance.*
>
> PROVERBS 11:14, CSB

In other words, when we try to navigate life on our own, we are more likely to stumble into traps we could have avoided. But when we surround ourselves with godly counselors—trusted friends, mentors, parents, and pastors—we give ourselves a safeguard against poor decisions and blind spots. Samson's story illustrates what happens when we elevate our feelings over wise guidance: His strength was wasted, his vision was lost, and his freedom was stolen.

The book of Titus instructs older men and women to teach/mentor the younger generation. Our question to you, then, is: Who are you mentoring and who is mentoring you? Are you only listening to the voices of other people who are at the same age and life stage as you? If so, you could rob yourself of growth and potential.

The significance of listening to wise counsel can be the difference between destruction and deliverance. The voices you allow to shape your direction are shaping your destiny. If Samson had listened, his story might have looked very different. And if we humble ourselves and listen, our story can too.

⚓ Anchor Point

A fool's way is right in his own eyes,
but whoever listens to counsel is wise.
PROVERBS 12:15, CSB

🕮 Ship Log (Reflection)

When did you ignore good advice and regret it? What would have changed if you'd listened?

🗨 Crew Talk (Discussion)

Who are you allowing to speak into your life—and where are they leading you?

Who are your "wise voices" right now? Who needs to be tuned out?

The Port of Application

Inspect Your Influences.

List the top voices shaping you. Are they wise?

Invert the Perspective.

Would you take your own advice? What needs to change so that others could?

Implore God for Wisdom.

Ask God for humble, teachable ears—and for counselors who point you to Him. Read Titus 2:1-8. God gives us specific instructions on who we should be listening to and what their lives should look like. List below the characteristics God desires to see in your life.

 Closing Prayer

Lord, thank You for placing wise people in my life. Help me to seek counsel that honors You and ignore voices that lead me astray. Give me a humble spirit and surround me with truth-tellers. In Jesus' name, Amen.

FOUR

The Ship of **CONCEALMENT**

SECRECY SINKS SHIPS, but integrity and accountability keep us afloat. When we recognize the enemy's traps, live with honesty, and invite others to walk alongside us, we can sail in freedom instead of fear.

The Hidden Cargo

The Ship of Concealment is a dangerous vessel because it rarely announces its arrival. It slips in silently, carrying hidden cargo—secrets that weigh heavily below the surface and eventually sink trust. Concealment thrives in the shadows, convincing us that no one will notice that we can manage it on our own, or that a little compromise won't hurt anyone. Yet history, experience, and Scripture all remind us that hidden sin is never harmless. From private addictions that erode integrity to quiet compromises that chip away at character, concealment has wrecked countless lives, families, and ministries.

Samson knew this struggle. He often lived with one foot in his calling and the other in his compromise. His strength was a gift from God, but he repeatedly concealed his weaknesses and indulged his desires in secret. Rather than bringing his struggles into the light where God's grace and accountability could have strengthened him, he tried to manage them alone. Eventually, what he thought he could hide became the very thing that undid him.

We see the same pattern today. A husband hides financial debt from his wife, convincing himself that he'll fix it before she ever finds out—until the bills come due and the trust collapses. A teenager deletes their online history to conceal unhealthy choices, all the while drifting further from the people who love them most. A leader buries bitterness or anger instead of dealing with it, and over time, it leaks out in destructive ways. The details may differ, but the result is the same: the hidden cargo becomes too heavy, and the ship begins to sink.

The good news is that God never calls us to live under the burden of hidden sin. He invites us to bring it into the light, to confess, to be healed, and to sail freely again. The Ship of Concealment doesn't have to define our journey if we're willing to unload the cargo and let God's forgiveness set us free.

Samson's Secret

Twice in Judges 14, Samson kept things from his parents. On his way to Timnah, he encountered a lion and later discovered its carcass with a swarm of bees and honey inside. Though his Nazirite vow required him to avoid anything dead, he scooped out the honey and ate it. Then, as if nothing had happened, he shared some with his parents—but he didn't tell them where it came from (Judges 14:6-9). It might seem like a minor detail, but it reveals something much bigger. Instead of being transparent, Samson chose secrecy. Instead of honoring his vow and confessing his failure, he concealed it.

Concealment often feels easier in the moment. It promises to protect our reputation, to keep the peace, or to help us avoid conflict. But in reality, it breeds stress, shame, and fear. The longer we hide something, the heavier the weight becomes. Samson may have thought he was keeping control, but secrecy was already loosening the foundation of his calling. What we keep hidden doesn't stay hidden forever. Eventually, it seeps into our relationships, erodes our integrity, and damages the trust others place in us.

Have you ever told a little white lie or hid something, thinking no one would ever find out? Maybe it was a secret purchase, a compromise at work, or a private struggle you convinced yourself you could manage. For a while, it may have felt harmless. But then came the fallout—a broken relationship, a damaged reputation, or a wave of guilt that was heavier than the secret itself. Samson's story reminds us that what we conceal in the dark will eventually surface, and often the cost is greater than we ever imagined.

Whoever conceals their sins does not prosper, but
the one who confesses and renounces them finds mercy.
PROVERBS 28:13 NIV

The good news is that God doesn't expose our secrets to shame us but to heal us. When we bring our hidden struggles into His light, we exchange secrecy for freedom, fear for peace, and shame for grace. Concealment may feel easier, but confession leads to life.

Three Life Preservers to Avoid Concealment

Look Out for the Enemy's Traps.

Jesus warned us clearly:

> *A thief comes only to steal and kill and destroy.*
> *I have come so that they may have life*
> *and have it in abundance.*
> JOHN 10:10, CSB

The enemy's goal is never for our good. His schemes are designed to rob us of joy, peace, and purpose. Peter adds another layer of urgency:

> *Be sober-minded, be alert. Your adversary the devil is*
> *prowling around like a roaring lion,*
> *looking for anyone he can devour.*
> 1 PETER 5:8, CSB

The devil doesn't come at us in obvious ways—he sets traps that look appealing, opportunities that look harmless, or secrets that seem manageable. The lie he whispers is, "No one will know." But the truth is that secrecy doesn't liberate us—it enslaves us. What begins as a private compromise often grows into a chain that weighs us down. Recognizing the enemy's tactics is the first step to staying free. We must stay alert, guard our hearts, and refuse to take the bait of concealment.

Live with Integrity.

Jesus gave a simple but powerful command:

But let your 'yes' mean 'yes,'
and your 'no' mean 'no.'
Anything more than this is from the evil one.
MATTHEW 5:37, CSB

Integrity means living without a double life. It means who you are in private matches who you are in public. That kind of consistency builds trust and protects us from the pull of concealment. But integrity doesn't happen by accident; it requires intentional guardrails. It might mean setting up shared accounts with your spouse, keeping your devices visible, having healthy boundaries in your friendships, or being transparent with finances. When we walk in transparency with others, we find freedom, strength, and healing.

Therefore, confess your sins to each other and pray for each other so that you may be healed. The prayer of a righteous person is powerful and effective.
JAMES 5:16 NIV

These steps don't restrict freedom; they safeguard it. Integrity is like a compass on a ship—it ensures you stay on course, even when the waves of temptation try to push you off track. When your words and actions consistently align with truth, there's no need to hide.

Let Yourself be Held Accountable.

Concealment thrives in isolation; accountability thrives in community. One of the enemy's greatest strategies is to convince us we can handle our struggles alone. But Scripture consistently calls us into relationships where we can be known, encouraged, and corrected. Accountability is not about control; it's about protection. It means inviting trusted people into your life and permitting them to ask difficult questions. It could be a spouse, a close friend, a mentor, or a small group, but the key is honesty and consistency. Accountability keeps us from drifting too far because someone else can spot the warning signs we might ignore.

Just as a ship needs both a crew and navigational tools to stay the course, we need others to help us avoid the dangers of concealment. When we walk in transparency with others, we find freedom, strength, and grace that secrecy can never provide.

The Hope of Honesty

What's hidden can be brought to light—not to shame you, but to heal you. God's heart is never to expose us to humiliation, but to free us from the chains that secrecy creates. Confession is not about punishment; it's about restoration. When we bring our hidden struggles into the light, we step into God's mercy, where forgiveness is waiting, and healing can begin. The burden of concealment is heavy, but honesty lifts the weight and opens the door to peace.

History gives us powerful reminders of this truth. Consider the story of President Abraham Lincoln. Throughout his life, he was known as "Honest Abe," a man whose integrity and transparency made him trustworthy in the eyes of the people. But Lincoln's honesty was not born out of ease; it was tested in difficulty. In his younger years as a lawyer, he developed a reputation for telling the truth even when it cost him a case or went against his own interests. Over time, that integrity became the very thing that gave him credibility to lead a divided nation through its darkest hour. His legacy reminds us that honesty may be costly in the short term, but it builds trust that outlasts generations.

The same is true for us. When we choose honesty, even about our failures, God can use it to strengthen relationships, rebuild trust, and demonstrate His grace to others. What once felt like a source of shame can become a testimony of redemption. The hope of honesty is that no matter how long we've carried hidden cargo, God is ready to meet us with forgiveness and give us the freedom to sail forward again.

If we confess our sins,
he is faithful and righteous to forgive us our sins
and to cleanse us from all unrighteousness.
1 JOHN 1:9, CSB

Honesty opens the door to God's forgiveness. Confession doesn't expose us to condemnation—it invites us into cleansing and freedom.

⚓ Anchor Point

Everything exposed by the light is made visible,
for what makes everything visible is light.
EPHESIANS 5:13-14A, CSB

🕮 Ship Log (Reflection)

What are you most tempted to hide? Write it down; pray for the courage to confess.

🗨 Crew Talk (Discussion)

Why do we hide? How can honesty rebuild trust in relationships?

The Port of Application

See the Wreckage.

Where has secrecy damaged trust in your life—or in someone else's you've observed?

Stay Honest.

Would you be comfortable with your spouse, parent, or closest friend seeing your digital life? Why or why not?

Seek Accountability.

Identify one person to invite into your struggle this week.

 Closing Prayer

Lord, help me live with honesty and integrity. Protect me from concealment's lies. Surround me with people who will hold me accountable and give me courage to walk in the light. In Jesus' name, Amen.

FIVE

The Ship of **CONSTRAINT**

SAILING THE SHIP of Constraint comes at a devastating price. We do not arrive there all at once; it begins with drifting—small compromises, ignored warnings, unwise associations. Slowly, the drift becomes a current that carries us where we never intended to go. What once felt like freedom turns out to be bondage. What once promised satisfaction becomes slavery. We find ourselves chained not by physical shackles, but by destructive habits, toxic relationships, shame from past mistakes, or patterns of sin that weigh us down.

Bound and Broken

Samson's story is one of the most dramatic reversals in all of Scripture. Once celebrated as the strongest man alive, he went from tearing lions apart with his bare hands and defeating armies with the jawbone of a donkey to being bound with bronze shackles, blinded, and forced to grind grain in humiliation like an ox.

His fall was not sudden; it was slow, subtle, and steady. Compromise after compromise eroded his calling. Misplaced trust in Delilah opened the door for betrayal. An unguarded weakness became the snare that cost him everything. The tragedy is summed up in a single verse:

> *The Philistines seized him and gouged out his eyes.*
> *They brought him down to Gaza and*
> *bound him with bronze shackles,*
> *and he was forced to grind grain in the prison.*
> JUDGES 16:21, CSB

The judge of Israel—chosen, empowered, and anointed by God to deliver His people—was now enslaved by the very enemies he had been called to conquer. The man who once struck fear into the Philistines now lived in chains, reduced to menial labor in prison.

Samson's story warns us that no amount of talent, strength, or calling can protect us if we continually choose compromise over obedience. But it also reminds us that God's story doesn't end in defeat. Even in prison, God was not finished with Samson. And the same is true for us. Constraint doesn't have to be the final chapter. [Read more on this in Chapter 7.]

Constrained by Place

Samson went down to Gaza, which was a Philistine stronghold, an enemy territory, and a place where he had no business being. It wasn't just a casual trip; it was a decision that placed him in direct proximity to temptation and danger. Being in the wrong place left him vulnerable, and that vulnerability eventually led to his captivity. Samson's downfall didn't begin with chains in a prison; it began with a choice of location. Where he positioned himself set the stage for his greatest defeat.

The same is true for us. The "places" we allow ourselves to dwell—physically, digitally, and even emotionally—have the power to shape our direction.

A physical place could be the environment we choose to spend time in, such as:

- The party we know will test our boundaries,
- A workplace that feeds unhealthy habits, or
- A relationship that constantly pulls us away from God.

A digital place might be the websites we visit, the shows we stream, or the social media accounts we follow. These spaces may seem harmless at first, but over time, they can erode our values and lure us into compromise.

Emotional places can be just as dangerous. Dwelling in bitterness, resentment, or comparison keeps us chained to negativity and blinds us from God's truth.

The reality is this: the *wrong* places rarely lead to *right* outcomes. If we continually place ourselves where temptation thrives, we shouldn't be surprised when we end up ensnared. Just as Samson discovered, stepping into enemy territory makes it that much easier for the enemy to step into us. But when we intentionally choose places that honor God, such as places of worship, community, encouragement, and accountability, we position ourselves for freedom, growth, and blessing.

Are you involved in a Bible-believing, Bible-preaching church? Do you have a Christian community surrounding you? If not, maybe it's time to take that first step. Find a church and community of believers that will help you grow and get involved. I (Teresa) found mine by just showing up at a BSM (Bible Study Ministry) for free food. I shudder at the thought of what my life might look like, 30 years later, if I had not taken the first step. So don't wait; find the right fellowSHIP for you!

Constrained by People

Samson gave Delilah repeated access to his heart, and she wore him down until he gave up his secret.

> *Because she nagged him day after day*
> *and pleaded with him until she wore him out,*
> *he told her the whole truth. . .*
> JUDGES 16:16-17A, CSB

Many of us have people in our lives who are like Delilah—pressuring, manipulating, or distracting us from God's best. Samson's downfall wasn't only about his physical strength being taken; it was also about the inner weakness of letting the wrong voice have control over his decisions. The wrong voices will always lead to the wrong choices.

In our world today, people-pleasing has become a disease. We care so much about making others happy, gaining approval, and avoiding conflict that we sacrifice our own peace and obedience to God. Like Samson, we can feel the constant pull to say "Yes" when we should say "No," or to compromise what we know is right because we don't want to disappoint someone else. The weight of that bondage leaves us drained, resentful, and empty.

I (Jon) know this struggle well because I have wrestled with being a people pleaser most of my life. I've often said "Yes" to commitments I didn't have the margin for, just because I didn't want to let someone down. I've gone out of my way to earn someone's approval, even when it meant neglecting my family or ignoring God's nudge in another direction. Deep down, I wanted to be liked, accepted, and seen as "the good guy." But the truth is, every time I gave in to that pressure, I ended up feeling more enslaved than fulfilled. The applause of people is fleeting, and it never satisfies the way obedience to Christ does.

To fill that void, Scripture calls us to shift our focus and live for an audience of one. Jesus is the only One worthy of our full devotion, because He has already done for us what no one else ever could. He laid down His life to save us, and He continues to walk with us, guide us, and sustain us in ways people never can.

When we stop striving to please everyone around us and instead fix our eyes on Him, we discover freedom. The same hands that bore the nails are the hands that hold us steady, and His approval is the only one that truly matters.

Constrained by Passions

Samson's greatest enemy wasn't the Philistines—it was his unchecked passions. Long before bronze shackles bound him, lust, pride, and anger had already chained him from the inside. His story is a sobering reminder that our greatest battles are often not with external enemies, but with the appetites of our own hearts.

Today, one of the most common areas where unchecked passion shows up is sexual temptation and pornography. Countless men and women silently struggle with it, often feeling trapped in cycles of secrecy, guilt, and shame. What begins as curiosity or an outlet can quickly become a snare that pulls people away from intimacy with God, damages relationships, and erodes their sense of purpose. Like Samson, we can think we're in control, but compromise will always lead to constraint.

Boundaries and guardrails are extremely vital. Guardrails may look like accountability software, honest conversations with trusted believers, or clear commitments about where we spend our time and attention. They're not about restriction—they're about protection. They help us avoid the traps that steal our freedom and keep us living in the calling God has for us.

For those wrestling with pornography or sexual brokenness, some faith-based tools and ministries can help bring hope and freedom:

- **Covenant Eyes** - This is accountability and filtering software to help create transparency, found at covenanteyes.com.

- **Fortify** - This is an app designed to provide biblical teaching, tools, and community for recovery found at www.joinfortify.com.
- **Focus on the Family** - This app offers Christ-centered articles, counseling referrals, and practical steps for individuals and families seeking healing. The app is located online at www.focusonthefamily.com.

The truth is, unchecked passions will always lead to bondage, but surrendered passions—placed in God's hands—can lead to freedom. The very heart of the Ship of Constraint is when we let our desires steer us and eventually bind us. But when we let Christ take the helm, we discover true freedom, purpose, and the abundant life God has promised.

Constrained by Pride

Samson assumed his strength would always remain, no matter how recklessly he lived. Pride blinded him long before the Philistines did.

Pride convinces us that we are invincible. It keeps us from confessing weakness and makes us think we can handle life alone. But unchecked pride always leads to a fall.

So, whoever thinks he stands
must be careful not to fall.
1 CORINTHIANS 10:12, CSB

Pride comes before destruction,
and an arrogant spirit before a fall.
PROVERBS 16:18, CSB

Both Scriptures highlight this point! Left to our devices and plans, we will fail because many times we think we're invincible or believe "it will never happen to me." Then it does. No one, to my knowledge, got in trouble for being humble. Still, plenty of people have been shipwrecked due to pride and its resulting destruction.

Constrained by Problems of the Heart

Samson's story reminds us that the greatest battles are often not on the outside but within. An "unprotected heart" is like an open door—it allows the enemy to step in and slowly tighten his grip. Samson's strength was unmatched, but his heart was vulnerable. He let pride, lust, and anger lead him instead of surrendering those desires to God. In the end, his external chains in Gaza were only a reflection of the internal chains he had carried for years. Scripture warns us plainly:

Guard your heart above all else,
for it is the source of life.
PROVERBS 4:23, CSB

The heart is the wellspring of our choices, motives, and desires. What flows out of it shapes the entire course of our lives. When we leave it unguarded, we give sin an opportunity to plant seeds that grow into regret and ruin. What we refuse to surrender to God will eventually shackle us—whether that's bitterness, unforgiveness, pride, or secret sin.

The truth is, many of us carry past mistakes and regrets like Samson carried his unchecked passions. We try to bury them deep, but instead they weigh us down with shame. Addictions, hidden habits, or wounds left unhealed can become chains that keep us from experiencing the freedom God intended. The Ship of Constraint doesn't always look like outward failure; sometimes it looks like it is smiling on the outside while silently drowning on the inside.

But here's the hope: what we release to Christ loses its power to enslave us. Jesus bore our shame on the cross, so we don't have to carry it anymore. Guarding our hearts means surrendering daily and choosing to let God cleanse, renew, and strengthen the very place where life begins. When we let Him take control of our hearts, the enemy loses his grip, and we discover the freedom to sail forward without chains.

⚓ Anchor Point

So if the Son sets you free, you really will be free.

JOHN 8:36, CSB

"...You will know the truth,
and the truth will set you free."

JOHN 8:32, CSB

For freedom, Christ set us free. Stand firm, then, and don't submit again to a yoke of slavery.
GALATIANS 5:1, CSB

🕮 Ship Log (Reflection)

What "places" do you need to avoid because they pull you away from God?

Which passions or patterns in your heart threaten to chain you?

What regret or failure from your past do you need to release to Christ?

Crew Talk (Discussion)

Share a time when you felt spiritually or emotionally bound. How did God begin setting you free?

Why do the wrong places and people so often appear appealing?

What role does community play in breaking chains of the past?

The Port of Application

Spot the Chains.

List three areas where you feel constrained, whether by a place, person, passion, pride, or past.

Search the Source.

Ask yourself: "Where is this coming from? Am I letting myself stay in the wrong place, around the wrong people, or under the wrong influence?"

Supplant the Lie.

Find a specific verse that speaks truth into that area (e.g., Galatians 5:1 for freedom, John 8:36 for release, Proverbs 4:23 for protection).

Step into Freedom.

Take one practical step this week to break free—set a boundary, confess to someone, change an environment, or surrender a regret to God.

Sustain this Activity Daily.

Freedom is not a one-time event; it's a daily choice to walk in truth rather than chains. Write out a prayer below that you can pray daily, using Scripture to overcome your constraints.

 Closing Prayer

Lord, I confess that I have allowed places, people, passions, pride, and my past to constrain me. Break the chains that bind me and lead me into the freedom that only You can give. Teach me to guard my heart, set wise boundaries, and rely on Your Spirit daily. Let my life be a testimony of Your power to set captives free. And use my freedom not only to bless me, but to bring hope to others who are still bound. In Jesus' name, Amen.

SIX

The Ship of **COMMITMENT**

WE LIVE IN a world where broken promises have become normal. We forgive the weatherman and keep watching, even when the forecast is wrong. We stay loyal to losing teams season after season, cheering them on despite their record. We even laugh at the pun that elevators will always "let us down."

But when it comes to the people closest to us—our spouse, family, friends—we often struggle to extend the same grace. Instead of patience, we hold on to hurt. Instead of loyalty, we nurse grudges. Instead of perseverance, we entertain the idea of walking away.

Why Commitment Feels Hard

Commitment feels hard because relationships require more than feelings; they require faithfulness. The Ship of Commitment can't sail on good intentions alone. For relationships to thrive, they must carry three essentials: **letting go, loving by forgiving, and living by faith.**

Letting Go

To remain committed, we must learn to release the baggage of past offenses. Carrying resentment is like loading extra weight onto a ship—it slows us down and eventually drags us under. When we cling to bitterness, replay old wounds, or constantly measure someone by their failures, we aren't just hurting the relationship; we're shackling ourselves. Letting go doesn't mean pretending the hurt never happened or minimizing the pain. Instead, it means making the intentional choice not to let that hurt define the relationship's future.

Samson's story gives us a glimpse of God's own heart. Samson broke his vows, squandered his calling, and gave in to compromise again and again. God could have given up on Samson—but He didn't. Even after Samson was blinded and bound in bronze shackles, God's mercy gave him one final opportunity to fulfill his calling. The Lord forgave and remained committed to him, proving that grace can still work through the broken. Scripture declares:

> *As far as the east is from the west,*
> *so far has he removed our transgressions from us.*
> PSALM 103:12, CSB

God shows us what true letting go looks like—He doesn't just forgive; He releases us from the weight of our past.

I've (Jon) watched this live out in Teresa. Over the years, she's had multiple so-called "friends" who hurt her deeply—through malicious words, betrayal, or actions that cut to the core. I've seen her grieve, sometimes with tears, sometimes with frustration. But what amazes me is how she doesn't stay stuck there. After a short season of hurt, she chooses to let it go. She doesn't excuse the wrong, but she refuses to let it define how she sees that person. Instead, she chooses to see them as Jesus sees them—a sinner saved by grace. I believe she can do this because she is continually reminded of all that Jesus has forgiven her for. Out of the overflow of that forgiveness, she freely forgives others.

And that same grace we've received is the grace we must extend to others. Jesus said:

Just as you want others to do for you,
do the same for them.
LUKE 6:31, CSB

We long for people to release our mistakes, to see us for who we are becoming instead of who we were. That means we must do the same. In relationships, commitment can only survive when forgiveness is practiced and grace is extended.

Letting go is not weakness—it's freedom. It's cutting away the ropes of resentment so that the Ship of Commitment can keep moving forward. It's saying, "I won't let yesterday's hurt steal tomorrow's joy." When we let go, we mirror the heart of God, and we create space for love, trust, and faith to flourish again.

Loving by Forgiving

Forgiveness is the anchor of the Ship of Commitment. Without it, no relationship can weather the storms of life. Every relationship—marriage, friendship, family, or even church community—will experience disappointment and offense because none of us is perfect. Love that doesn't forgive cannot last. But love that chooses to forgive creates space for healing, growth, and deeper trust.

Samson's life again shows us the consequences of failing to forgive. His story is marked by cycles of offense and revenge. When the Philistines wronged him, he struck back in anger. When he felt betrayed, he responded with violence. Instead of releasing his hurt, he allowed bitterness and vengeance to steer his decisions. That path led only to destruction. By contrast, Jesus modeled a better way. Hanging on the cross, abandoned by His friends and mocked by His enemies, He prayed:

Then Jesus said, "Father, forgive them,
because they do not know what they are doing."
LUKE 23:34A, CSB

Jesus chose forgiveness, even in His greatest pain, and He calls us to do the same. Scripture reminds us:

And be kind and compassionate to one another,
forgiving one another,
just as God also forgave you in Christ.
EPHESIANS 4:32, CSB

Forgiveness is not optional for followers of Jesus—it's central to who we are. We forgive not because people deserve it, but because we've been forgiven far more than we could ever repay. As Paul writes in Colossians:

Just as the Lord has forgiven you,
so you are also to forgive.
COLOSSIANS 3:13B, CSB

In today's world, forgiveness may be one of the hardest acts of love. Spouses carry wounds from harsh words. Friends grow distant over betrayal. Families are divided by years of resentment. Yet the call remains: forgive as you have been forgiven. That doesn't mean ignoring pain or trusting recklessly, but it does mean releasing the offense to God, refusing to let bitterness be the lens through which we view others.

True commitment requires forgiveness. Without it, relationships become prisons of past mistakes. With it, they become pictures of grace. To love by forgiving is to reflect the very heart of Christ—the One who forgave us first, and who continues to forgive us daily.

Living by Faith

Feelings do not fuel commitment; feelings are sustained by faith. Feelings rise and fall like waves, but faith steadies the ship when the storm threatens to overwhelm. To live by faith means to trust that God is working even when we don't see it, to believe that His purposes are unfolding even when our circumstances look bleak, and to anchor our relationships in His promises, rather than our own strength.

Samson's life looked like a failure. From a human perspective, his story ends in shame—blinded, bound, and grinding grain in the prison of his enemies. And yet, Scripture surprises us. Hebrews 11, often called the "Hall of Faith," lists Samson among the heroes:

And what more can I say?
Time is too short for me to tell about
Gideon, Barak, Samson, Jephthah,
David, Samuel, and the prophets,
HEBREWS 11:32, CSB

Despite his failures, Samson is remembered not for his flaws but for the faith he demonstrated at the end of his life. Blinded and broken, he prayed:

He called out to the LORD,
"Lord GOD, please remember me.
Strengthen me, God, just once more. . ."
JUDGES 16:28A, CSB

Samson's prayer wasn't a polished one. It wasn't eloquent. It was raw, honest, and desperate. And God answered. In his final act, Samson brought down the temple of the Philistines, fulfilling his calling to deliver Israel. His life reminds us that faith isn't about perfection—it's about direction. It's not about how polished our words sound, but where we place our trust.

In our own lives, the same truth applies. Living by faith means trusting God with our marriages when they feel fragile, believing He can heal friendships that seem broken beyond repair, and relying on Him to carry us through seasons when commitment feels impossible. Faith says, "I don't have to see the whole picture to trust the One who does."

The question isn't if you have faith, but where you place it. If you place your faith in yourself, in circumstances, or in other people, disappointment is inevitable. But when your faith is anchored in Christ, your commitment can endure because it rests on the One who is faithful even when we are not.

The Ship of Commitment is not easy to sail. The waters are rough, the storms are real, and the temptation to abandon the ship is strong. But by **letting go, loving by forgiving, and living by faith**, we can stay the course. Commitment isn't about perfection—it's about choosing daily to trust God, extend grace, and remain anchored in His love.

It means refusing to let temporary feelings decide the long-term direction of our relationships. It means clinging to the hope that God can redeem what feels broken and breathe life into what seems beyond repair. And when we do, our relationships reflect the faithfulness of the One who never lets us go, showing the world a glimpse of Christ's unshakable love.

⚓ Anchor Point

And be kind and compassionate to one
another, forgiving one another,
just as God also forgave you in Christ.

EPHESIANS 4:32, CSB

📖 Ship Log (Reflection)

Write your version of Samson's prayer. Where do you need God's strength "just once more?"

Crew Talk (Discussion)

How do small acts of forgiveness keep commitment alive in relationships?

The Port of Application

Who Do You Need to Forgive?

Reflect on how much unforgiveness has cost you.

What Action Can You Take?

Choose one small, loving act this week.

Where's Your Faith?

Journal a prayer naming the area where you need God's strength.

 Closing Prayer

Lord, thank You for being committed to me even when I fail. Help me to let go, forgive, and live by faith. "Lord God, please remember me. Strengthen me just once more." Restore what's broken. In Jesus' name, Amen.

SEVEN

The Ship of **CLEAN SLATE**

BOARDING THE SHIP of Clean Slate requires surrender and faith. Surrender means admitting we can't fix ourselves or erase our own mistakes. Faith means believing that Jesus' death and resurrection are enough—that His grace covers our past and His Spirit empowers our future.

Starting Over

From playground "do-overs" to video game restarts, there's something deep in the human heart that longs for a second chance. As kids, we called it a "redo." As adults, we talk about fresh starts or new chapters. Whether it's a broken relationship, a decision we regret, or a sin that weighs heavily on our conscience, we crave a clean slate. That longing is not accidental—it's spiritual. God designed us with a need for renewal, and He provided the ultimate way to experience it through Jesus Christ.

Samson's story is a powerful picture of this truth. By the time we reach Judges 16, Samson looks like a man whose story is over. The strongest man in Israel is now blind, bound in bronze shackles, and grinding grain like a slave. The hero who once struck fear in the Philistines is reduced to humiliation. From the outside, it looked like his failures had disqualified him forever. But God wasn't finished with Samson. Even in the ruins of his mistakes, the Ship of Clean Slate was waiting in port.

The Ship of Clean Slate is available to us, always in port—its fare already paid in full by the blood of Jesus. Scripture promises:

> *Because of the LORD's faithful love*
> *we do not perish, for his mercies never end.*
> *They are new every morning;*
> *great is your faithfulness!*
> LAMENTATIONS 3:22–23, CSB

Every sunrise is proof that God still offers fresh mercy, no matter how badly we've failed.

Samson's story shows us that starting over doesn't mean our history disappears—it means God can use even our failures as part of His redemption story.

If Samson, blinded and broken, could find a clean slate through one prayer of faith, then so can we. No matter how far we've drifted, the Ship of Clean Slate is ready to carry us into freedom.

Therefore, if anyone is in Christ,
he is a new creation;
the old has passed away,
and see, the new has come!
2 CORINTHIANS 5:17, CSB

The Person at the Helm

Samson, at his lowest moment, cried out to God:

He called out to the LORD, "Lord GOD, please remember me. Strengthen me, God, just once more. With one act of vengeance, let me pay back the Philistines for my two eyes." Samson took hold of the two middle pillars supporting the temple and leaned against them, one on his right hand and the other on his left. Samson said, "Let me die with the Philistines." He pushed with all his might, and the temple fell on the leaders and all the people in it. And those he killed at his death were more than those he had killed in his life.
JUDGES 16:28–30, CSB

Samson's desperate prayer was directed at the true Captain of his life. In that final moment, he recognized that his strength did not come from himself, but from the Lord who had called him from birth. Even in his brokenness, even in his blindness, Samson entrusted the helm of his ship back to the One who had been guiding it all along.

That cry of surrender reminds us that no matter how far we have strayed or how deeply we have failed, we can still call on God—and He still hears. Today, we know His name—Jesus.

Jesus told him, "I am the way,
the truth, and the life.
No one comes to the Father except through me."
JOHN 14:6, CSB

History itself pivots on His life. His once-fearful disciples, who ran and hid when He was arrested, became bold witnesses after seeing Him risen. These ordinary men and women chose torture, imprisonment, and even death rather than denying Him. They weren't defending a myth or an idea—they were proclaiming a person they had seen with their own eyes, touched with their own hands, and heard with their own ears.

When Jesus is at the helm, everything changes. He doesn't just give us directions from the shore; He steps onto the deck and takes control of the wheel. He steers us through storms, corrects our drifting, and brings us safely into harbor. The question is: Who is at the helm of your ship? Are you still clinging to the wheel, convinced you can chart your own course? Or have you surrendered control to Jesus, the Captain who not only knows the way, but *is* the Way?

The Plea Must be Made

Like Samson, we too must cry out. He asked God to remember him and strengthen him—and God responded. His story shows us that

God is ready to hear us, but we must call on Him in faith. Scripture makes this clear:

> *If you confess with your mouth, "Jesus is Lord,"*
> *and believe in your heart that God raised*
> *him from the dead, you will be saved.*
> *One believes with the heart,*
> *resulting in righteousness,*
> *and one confesses with the mouth,*
> *resulting in salvation.*
> ROMANS 10:9–10, CSB

Redemption and grace through faith in Jesus Christ are the heart of the gospel. To have the peace of knowing Jesus as your personal Lord and Savior, you must take action. It begins with acknowledging your sin and asking Him to forgive you. It means believing that Jesus is the Messiah—the Son of God—who died on the cross to pay the price for your sins and rose again in victory. And it requires committing your life to Him, allowing Him to take the helm and direct your course.

The good news is that this plea never falls on deaf ears. It reaches the God who formed you, loves you, and has been waiting for you to come home. Salvation isn't about being good enough or cleaning yourself up first—it's about surrendering your heart to the One who already paid it all. When you confess and believe, Jesus not only forgives your past but secures your future, giving you the peace and assurance that you belong to Him forever.

The Power to Change Must be Understood

God answered Samson's final prayer dramatically, turning his weakest moment into his greatest victory.

Samson said, "Let me die with the Philistines."
He pushed with all his might, and the temple
fell on the leaders and all the people in it.
And those he killed at his death were more
than those he had killed in his life.
JUDGES 16:30, CSB

In human terms, Samson's story should have ended in defeat—blinded, humiliated, and chained as a slave to his enemies. But when he cried out to God, Heaven responded. What looked like the end became the moment where God displayed His strength most clearly. Samson's failure did not have the final word; God's power did. That same power is available to us today.

Now to him who is able to do above and beyond
all that we ask or think according to the power
that works in us—to him be glory in the church
and in Christ Jesus to all generations,
forever and ever. Amen.
EPHESIANS 3:20–21, CSB

Jesus Christ is the same
yesterday, today, and forever.
HEBREWS 13:8, CSB

The same God who restored Samson's strength is the God who restores broken marriages, heals fractured friendships, delivers from addiction, and renews lives that feel beyond repair. His power is not reserved for Bible heroes—it is living and active in every believer through the Holy Spirit.

The truth is, no relationship, mistake, or story is beyond His restoring power. What feels like the rubble of failure can become the foundation of a new testimony. What the enemy meant for destruction, God can use for redemption. But just as Samson had to humble himself and cry out, we too must recognize our weakness and invite God's strength to work within us. His power doesn't just patch up what's broken; it transforms it into something that brings Him glory.

The Greatest Invitation

The Ship of Clean Slate isn't just about starting over—it's about starting with Him. God offers the greatest invitation ever given: the chance to become His child and live in relationship with Him. Scripture tells us:

But to all who did receive him,
he gave them the right to be children of God,
to those who believe in his name,
JOHN 1:12, CSB

God's invitation is not earned by good works but received through faith. Paul makes it clear in the following verse:

For you are saved by grace through faith,
and this is not from yourselves; it is God's gift—
not from works, so that no one can boast.
EPHESIANS 2:8-9, CSB

It's a promise available to every single person.

For everyone who calls on
the name of the Lord will be saved.
ROMANS 10:13, CSB

And it comes with a breathtaking exchange:

For the wages of sin is death, but the gift of
God is eternal life in Christ Jesus our Lord.
ROMANS 6:23, CSB

The opportunity to trade guilt for grace, sin for Salvation, and death for everlasting life with Christ is the invitation of a lifetime. It's as simple as **A-B-C**:

A: Admit Your Sin.

The first step toward a clean slate is honesty. We all have areas where we've fallen short of God's standard. Scripture says:

For all have sinned
and fall short of the glory of God;
ROMANS 3:23, CSB

Admitting your sin does not mean wallowing in guilt. It means acknowledging your need for forgiveness. Just like a doctor can't treat an illness you refuse to admit you have, God cannot heal what you continue to hide. Confession opens the door for His mercy to rush in. Write down specific areas where you know you need God's forgiveness and pray over them one by one.

B: Believe in Jesus.

Faith isn't just intellectual agreement; it's trust. Believing means staking your life on who Jesus is and what He's done. He died on the cross to pay the penalty for your sin and rose again to give you new life.

Scripture reminds us:

If you confess with your mouth, "Jesus is Lord,"
and believe in your heart that God raised him
from the dead, you will be saved.
ROMANS 10:9, CSB

Believing in Jesus as your Lord and Savior is personal. It's not enough to say, "my parents believed" or "my church believes." Do you believe that Jesus died for you? Take a moment to reflect on the cross.

Imagine your sins nailed there with Him. Then imagine the empty tomb—and know that resurrection life is now yours through faith.

C: Commit Your Life to Him.

Salvation is not just about avoiding judgment; it is about entering a relationship. To commit is to surrender control—to hand Jesus the steering wheel of your life. Paul wrote:

Therefore, brothers and sisters,
in view of the mercies of God,
I urge you to present your bodies as a living sacrifice,
holy and pleasing to God; this is your true worship.
ROMANS 12:1, CSB

Commitment is daily. It means aligning your choices, priorities, and relationships with His Word. It may require letting go of old habits, walking away from toxic influences, or stepping boldly into new opportunities He calls you to. Begin small: pray each morning, "Lord, today I am Yours. Lead me, and I will follow."

If you are ready to receive the gift of Salvation today, pray the simple prayer shown below:

Lord Jesus, I know that I am a sinner and that I cannot save myself. I believe that You are the Son of God, that You died on the cross for my sins, and that You rose again so I could have eternal life. Today, I ask You to forgive me of my sins, come into my heart, and be my Lord and Savior. I commit my life to You from this day forward. Thank You for saving me and giving me a new beginning. In Your name I pray, Amen.

⚓ Anchor Point

God's grace writes new stories on broken pages. In Christ, failure is never final—every ending can become a new beginning.

🕮 Ship Log (Reflection)

Take time today to reflect on areas of your life where you long for a clean slate. Write down one relationship, one regret, or one habit you need to surrender to God. Beside it, write the words: "His mercies are new every morning" (Lamentations 3:23). Pray over each one, asking the Lord to redeem your past and lead you into His new beginning.

🗨 Crew Talk (Discussion)

Samson's story shows us that God can use even our failures for His glory. Can you think of a time when God redeemed something in your life that felt broken beyond repair?

What does it mean to you personally to let Jesus take the helm of your life? Have you ever done that? And if not, do you want to now?

If this is the first time you have prayed to commit your life to Christ, share it with your "crew" so they can encourage and pray for you.

How can this group (your "crew") encourage one another to live daily in the reality of a clean slate through Christ?

If this is the first time you have prayed to commit your life to Christ, share the news with your "crew" so they may encourage you and pray for you.

The Port of Application

Accept the Invitation.

Jesus has already paid the price for your clean slate. Yet many of us carry guilt, shame, or regret that He has already covered. Ask yourself: "Am I still holding on to something Christ has already nailed to the cross?" Spend a few moments in prayer, surrendering that weight to Him. Write it down in a journal as a reminder of what you've released.

Did you accept Jesus' invitation to receive him as personal Lord and Savior? If so, write this date down and remember this date as your "new birthday," the day you became a new creation in Christ.

Apply it Personally.

A clean slate is not just a theological truth—it's meant to transform your daily life. What is one specific area where you need a fresh start? Maybe it's your marriage, your parenting, your thought life, or even how you spend your time. Be honest with yourself and with God. Then, take one practical step this week that reflects your new beginning—whether it's having a needed conversation, setting a new boundary, or beginning a new habit.

Act with Grace.

Receiving grace should overflow into extending grace. Who in your life needs a clean slate from you? Forgiveness doesn't mean forgetting, but it does mean releasing the grip of bitterness. Think of one relationship where you can take a step toward reconciliation—whether by offering kind words, letting go of an old score, or simply praying a blessing over that person. Your willingness to extend grace may open the door for healing you never thought possible.

Closing Prayer

Jesus, I need Your grace. Thank You for paying my fare. I surrender my past and receive Your forgiveness. Make me new and teach me to extend a clean slate to others. Amen.

Workbook/Journal Questions

A Companion Guide to RelationSHIPS

Use these for personal reflection, journaling, or group discussion.

Chapter 1—The Ship of Calling

- What passions or burdens keep surfacing in your life?
- What fears or excuses have held you back from pursuing God's call?
- Write a prayer asking God to clarify your purpose and give you courage to step into it.

Chapter 2—The Ship of Catch

- What "hooks" or temptations tend to catch you?
- When have appearances led you astray?
- What boundary will you set this week to protect your heart?

Chapter 3—The Ship of Counsel

- List the three voices that most shape your decisions. Are they wise?

- Would you take counsel from yourself? Why or why not?

- Ask God to bring wise mentors and give you humility to listen.

Chapter 4—The Ship of Concealment

- What are you tempted to hide–and why?

- How has concealment damaged trust in your life (or in others' lives)?

- Who can you invite into honest accountability this week?

Chapter 5—The Ship of Constraint

- What "places" (physical/online) are danger zones for you?

- Who constrains your growth–and who frees it?

- Which heart issue do you need God to heal first?

Chapter 6—The Ship of Commitment

- Who do you need to forgive–and what has unforgiveness cost you?
- What loving action will you take this week to mend a relationship?
- Write your version of Samson's prayer: "Lord God, please remember me. Strengthen me just once more."

Chapter 7—The Ship of Clean Slate

- Do you believe Jesus has given you a clean slate? Why or why not?
- Where do you need a fresh start today?
- Who needs grace from you–and what step will you take?

About the Authors

Jon and Teresa Harper have spent nearly three decades navigating the waters of life together, learning firsthand that every relationship is a ship on a journey. Raised in very different family environments—one shaped by divorce and the other by a marriage that endured nearly fifty years—they understand that no two journeys look the same. But one thing is certain: All relationships require direction, care, and intentional navigation to reach their intended destination.

Through calm seas and unexpected storms, the Harpers have discovered that healthy *RelationSHIPS* don't drift—they are built. Whether it's marriage, parenting, friendships, leadership, or faith-based connections, strong relationships demand commitment, communication, and a shared willingness to grow. This conviction fuels their passion to help people in every stage of life learn how to stay the course, weather the storms, and arrive stronger together.

With over 29 years in ministry and 18 years of traveling and speaking across the United States, Jon and Teresa have impacted thousands through conferences, retreats, weekend events, camps, churches, and large-scale gatherings. Their messages are practical, engaging, and hope-filled—designed to meet people where they are and equip them with tools to build lasting, meaningful connections. The Harpers are available to speak at a wide variety of events, tailoring each message to fit the audience and setting.

Jon and Teresa live in Willis, Texas. They are the proud parents of three adult children who are thriving in their own marriages and dating relationships. They also enjoy spending time with their precious grandson as often as possible.

To learn more about the Harpers or to inquire about booking them for an event, visit **thewordministries.net**. For ongoing relationship encouragement, follow them on social media at:

TheWORDMinistries and **Minute4Marriage**

www.ingramcontent.com/pod-product-compliance
Lightning Source LLC
LaVergne TN
LVHW010934110826
845149LV00013B/2593

* 9 7 8 1 9 6 1 6 4 1 4 6 4 *